Contents

Speaking of Jane Roberts

Remembering
the Author of the
Seth Material

Susan M. Watkins

Moment Point Press
Portsmouth, New Hampshire

Moment Point Press, Inc.
P.O. Box 4549
Portsmouth, NH 03802-4549
www.momentpoint.com

Cover design by Metaglyph
Typeset in Goudy
MG

Portions of "The Flood, and What Washed Up There" originally appeared in the *Observer*, Dundee, New York.

The Strange Case of the Chestnut Beads appeared in somewhat different form as "Where Did Sue Watkins Really Come From?" in *Reality Change* magazine.

Library of Congress Cataloging-in-Publication Data

Watkins, Susan M., 1945–
    Speaking of Jane Roberts : remembering the
        author of the Seth material/Susan M. Watkins.
        p.cm.
    Includes bibliographical references and index.
    ISBN 0-9661327-7-7 (alk. paper)
        1. Roberts, Jane, 1929–84   2. Psychics—New York—Biography
        I. Title

BF1027. R62 W37 2001
133. 9'1'092—dc21
[B]   00-061283
Printed in the United States of America

10 9 8 7 6 5 4 3 2 1

In Memory of Tim Hilts

Also by Susan M. Watkins

Conversations with Seth

Dreaming Myself, Dreaming a Town

Garden Madness